Cobweb ... scue

Written by Daphne Faunce~Brown
Illustrated by Lynne Byrnes

Just like you Christopher!

Published by Studio Publications (Ipswich) Limited.
32, Princes Street, Ipswich IP1 1RJ
 Printed in Great Britain.

COBWEB and Wellington were picnicking at Tadpole Creek when they heard Jasper Toad calling to them.

"Would you two like some cress for your sandwiches?"

Wellington, who loved watercress, didn't even stop to think. He dashed across the stepping-stones towards Jasper.

Wellington had not realised that rubber boots slip when they are wet! As he landed on the first wet stone, his one hundred legs shot from under him.

SPLASH! Wellington was up to his nose in water and Wellington *hated* to be wet!

"Help, Jasper! Help me, I'm sinking!" he cried.

"Calm down, calm down," said Jasper, who loved water himself and couldn't understand the fuss. "How can you sink when you are already on the bottom?"

"Easily," replied Wellington crossly, as he felt his boots sinking deeper and deeper in the mud!

When Cobweb joined Jasper on the stepping-stones, he told Wellington to reach up with his front legs so that they could pull him out.

They tugged and they pulled and they pulled and they tugged and quite suddenly, Wellington shot out of the water. But without a single boot!

The three of them stared anxiously at the water, waiting for the boots to surface. All they saw was bubbles!

Wellington was near to tears as they walked home. "All those lovely boots that you had painted for me, Cobweb. Gone for ever. Not a boot to my name!"

When the friends got home, Wellington fetched his large money-jar. They use acorns and fir-cones as money; one hundred acorns equal one fir cone! Boots cost one acorn each (or two acorns for a pair!)

Wellington's jar had eighty acorns inside!

Cobweb, who was good at sums, said they needed to earn twenty more acorns.

"But how?" asked Wellington, who was hating the thought of a wet day without boots.

Cobweb suggested a sale. Lettuces and radishes on one stall and jumble on another.

"You could manage without at least three scarves for a start," suggested Cobweb.

"I suppose it is an emergency," said Wellington, none too pleased with the idea.

"I've made some 'sale' posters, Wellington," said Cobweb later that day. "You sort some things out for the stalls and I'll go and pin them up."

By two o'clock the following day, there was a long queue at Wellington's gate.

The friends were amazed and delighted to see how quickly everything sold. All Wellington's friends wanted to help for they knew how miserable he would be as long as he was bootless!

Cobweb caught one of the weasels up to his old tricks, stealing a scarf. The weasel left smiling wickedly, having no idea that he was, in fact, losing what he had taken!

Wellington made forty acorns from his sale. The twenty needed for his boots, ten to save in his money-jar and ten over.

They decided to leave the shopping until the following day. It takes a very long time to try on fifty pairs of boots!

Can you guess what the extra ten acorns were used for?

Yes, paint! So that Cobweb could make the new boots as colourful as the old ones!

As far as Cobweb knows, his old boots are still stuck in the mud at the bottom of Tadpole Creek!